WHEN YOUR LOVED ONE IS DYING

WHEN YOUR LOVED ONE IS DYING

Earl A. Grollman

BEACON PRESS
BOSTON

Copyright © 1980 by Earl A. Grollman
Beacon Press books are published under the auspices
of the Unitarian Universalist Association
Published simultaneously in Canada by
Fitzhenry & Whiteside Limited, Toronto
All rights reserved
Printed in the United States of America

(hardcover) 9 8 7 6 5 4 3 2 1

Library of Congress Cataloging in Publication Data

Grollman, Earl A
  When your loved one is dying.

    1. Death—Social aspects—United States.   2. Death—Psychological
aspects—United States.   3. Terminally ill—Family relationships.
4. Physician and patient.
I. Title.
HQ1073.5.U6G76   1980   155.9'37   79–3780
ISBN 0–8070–3216–6

In memory of Saul Lipton

Contents

*A man's dying
is more the
survivor's affair
than his own.*
THOMAS MANN, *The Magic Mountain*

What this book is about . . .

Someone in your family or a close friend is suffering from an illness or an injury that will be fatal. This has a compelling disruptive effect not only on the dying, but on the living as well.

You may say: "I couldn't imagine it could be like this."

The purpose of this book is to assist you in moving from helplessness to helpfulness; to help you cope with your own emotional upheaval, and better understand the needs of your loved one.

I. IMPACT AND GRIEF—When Your Loved One Is Dying

If you want life,
expect pain.
　　　　　—MARTIN BUBER

Your loved one is dying.

You feel as though you have fallen
into a dark pit,
separated from everyone and everything.

My God, my God,
  Why hast Thou forsaken me?
  I cry by day,
  but Thou dost not answer,
  and by night,
  but find no rest.
                                    —PSALMS

Time stands still.
The real seems so unreal.

You want to cry out.
But your throat is tight.

Your lips move.
But no sound comes forth.

Your body is frozen.

A huge stone has settled in
your stomach.

Gradually,
emotions rush over you,
invading and holding you
in the grip of
anger and anguish,
fear and frustration,
dread and despair.

You are afraid
you will lose control,
be swept away by
overpowering emotions.

You keep repeating:

"My loved one is dying.
My loved one is dying.
My loved one is dying."

as if the sounds
of these frightening words
will enable you to
understand and accept

the terrifying truth.

But
speech brings
little comfort or consolation.

You are in
excruciating pain.

The sting of impending death
is real.

Death is *so* final.

The thought of death
squeezes the life out of you.

The more your life is bound up
with your beloved
the more vulnerable you are
to grief.

You can't imagine living
without your loved one.

There is so much you *still* want to
share.

Dreams come crashing down.

"I wish God would take me instead."

Why pretend that you are not experiencing
difficult feelings
during the painful moments?

Is it because you are ashamed
of your vulnerability?

Is it because
raw honesty embarrasses you?

Have you been taught
to be strong,
not to show feelings?

It is *normal* to grieve,
anticipating the death of a loved one.

It's like losing a part of your self.

You have
a deep personal investment in your relationship.

You don't want to lose it
or your loved one.

Grief is an adaptive
response to loss.

And it begins *before* death.

Social scientists call it
"anticipatory" or "preparatory grief"—
the working through of your sorrow
as a rehearsal for death.

Your anticipation and preparation
help you to
understand and cope
with the impact of loss, and

to adjust to death
when it happens.

You have every right
to feel this anticipatory grief.

You may need to grieve ahead of time
over the ultimate losses
which must come
when your loved one dies.

You feel like a victim
of a sudden windstorm—
swept away by forces
you didn't expect and
can't control.

Not everyone will understand
your needs.

Some people may say to you,
"Don't be depressed,"
    or
"Don't act so angry."

Some people will
feel uncomfortable
with your frustration and rage.

But rest assured:
Your grief is a normal process
of waves and sensations,
which spin you around
in an emotional whirlpool.

How you confront your feelings
depends upon

the way you normally handle stress,
the pain of your impending loss, and
the support of your friends
and family.

Even though grief is
a common human experience,
it is as individual
as fingerprints—
appearing in
widely varying combinations.

As you experience
some of the emotions associated
with grief,
you may feel like a cork bobbing erratically
on a sea of conflicting emotions.

UNREALITY

You hear the words of loss
but don't feel them.

You cry in a detached way
devoid of any sense
of what is happening
to your loved one
and to you.

You feel numb.

An initial phase of grief
is a sense of unreality,
serving as a built-in buffer
to help you
weather the eye of the storm.

Numbness affords a respite—
an emotional suspension—
before you go forward
to accept the crunching news
that your loved one
is actually dying.

DISBELIEF

If you accept reality,
you might have to exchange
your numbness for pain.

It's hard to accept things
you don't want to be true,
to cope in the face of loss.

   "I *can't* believe it."
   "I *won't* believe it."
   "I *don't* believe it."

"There might be some mistake.
The medical reports are mixed up
with someone else's.

We'll get a second opinion
   —or a third—

There *must* be something
they can do."

You dream at night,
that your loved one is healthy,
just fine.

You take every small improvement
as a sign that your loved one
will get better.
"God wouldn't let this
happen to me *now!*"

Just as you may close your eyes
when something offends your sight,
so are you now refusing to accept

what your mind knows to be true.

Denial isn't
an all or nothing affair.

You may have moments of acceptance
when you think about the funeral
and your future—*alone.*

Alternately,
there could be complete repudiation
as you plan for
the far-off future—*together.*

> *Neither the sun nor death*
> *can be looked at*
> *with a steady eye.*
> —LA ROCHEFOUCAULD

Fantasies make acceptance
a slow process.

But eventually you will be able to say,
"My loved one is very sick
and will die."

This admission is a
landmark
in your journey.

PANIC

Acceptance, though, doesn't always
bring peace.
"Why can't I get hold of myself?"

Your physical and emotional
resources are overtaxed.

You feel like
you are losing control.

You feel helpless and disorganized.

"If only I could run away,
anywhere."

But your loved one *will* get worse.

You need time to
collect yourself.

HOSTILITY

When
  a mother's beauty fades,
  a strong father becomes frail,
  a child's hair falls out,

your sense of helplessness may turn to rage.

 "Why me?
  Why my beloved?
  What did *we* do to deserve this?"

You may be infuriated with
the doctors and nurses
  for not doing more,
the clergy,
  whose divine intervention has failed,
God,
  for being unjust,
friends and neighbors,
  who seem healthy and happy.

You may even be angry with your loved one,
who will die and
leave you behind.

And you are furious with yourself
for feeling furious.

Your nerves are constantly on edge.
Little things disturb you.

Anger comes unexpectedly and
is hard to contain.
You feel a lingering bitterness.

"I don't deserve this."

Rage
helps you to release
your anguish and frustration
at the curtailment of a life so precious to you,
and at your inability
to *do* something about it.

> *Do not go gentle into that good night!*
> *Rage, rage against the dying of the light.*
> —DYLAN THOMAS

Holding back your anger too much
can lead to a deep depression.

DEPRESSION

Your emotions are tamped down.
You have the sickening feeling
of going down, down, down.

Silence in solitude
is preferable to the burden of
socializing with friends.

You feel overwhelmed—drained.

Nothing matters anymore.
Nothing.

"Life will *never* be worth living."

Depression colors
everything you do and think.

Hopelessness
hangs around your neck,
like an albatross.

Every cloud does *not* have a silver lining.
When there is inner turmoil,
no cloud has a silver lining.

> *The grief that does not speak*
> *whispers the o'erfraught heart and*
> *bids it break.*
>   —SHAKESPEARE

Depression is anger turned inward,
a kind of frozen rage.

It is not only a normal response to anticipated loss,
but a psychological necessity
for working through your pain.

Now you are facing reality.
You are suffering.
The truth *has* registered.
The signs are impossible to ignore.
Your loved one *will* die.

And you have started to mourn.

BARGAINING

You no longer deny your loved one will die.
But *maybe* you can stave it off,
if you make a deal.

"I'll be more charitable.
Read the Bible.
Give up smoking.

Just let my beloved live
until
an anniversary . . . a graduation . . . a wedding.

I'll never ask another favor again."

These bargains, usually kept secret,
are your attempt to
improve the terms
of a contract with
destiny, fate, or God.

As a reward for your good behavior,
death will be postponed.

You hope.

Magical agreements have nothing
to do with the sickness
or health
of another person.

Even if you keep your
promises (and most people don't),
you can't put off the
inevitable.

Games people play:
"You die when your time is up."
"You're doing so well."
"Let's not talk about it."
"You'll live to be a hundred."

Avoidance, fatalism, changing the subject,
denial, reassurance—
all erect barriers to communication.

Games are usually played
for the survivors' sake,
not for the dying person.

Your loved one probably knows
more than you think.

You communicate
so much nonverbally.

You disclose information
by
facial expressions,
your mood,
defensiveness, and
avoidance.

Patients may learn of their conditions
from cues by the hospital staff
ranging in subtlety from
nurses' anxious glances and avoidance to
overhearing a discussion of the case
by doctors
outside the doorway.

Patients often sneak a glance
at their progress reports.

Nor are they fooled about
drastic changes in their bodies.

They know that
radical surgery
is not performed for trivial reasons, and
radiation therapy
is not administered for benign diseases.

They are not unthinking
    because
they are dying.

Even children sense fairly accurately
the trend of their illness.

They know they are deteriorating
when they have less
energy,
appetite,
enthusiasm.

Through their drawings and behavior
they let *us* know
that something traumatic
is happening to them.

Dying children use symbolic language
to reveal their inner concerns.

A little girl expressed her separation anxiety
by drawing a picture of a child
locked in a room.

A boy with leukemia
painted a small child in a boat,
crashing into the rocks,
sinking.

Another youngster drew a picture
of a crib
that looked like a prison.

When dying people of all ages
do not share their feelings and fears vocally,
their silence may not be denial of death,

but the attempt to conceal their awareness
from friends and family
they believe *can't* handle
an emotional confrontation,

and even from doctors and nurses
who might become annoyed and irritable.

The dying person becomes the
protector and caretaker
of the healthy.

What a burden that must be!

Your loved one
probably wants to know the truth.

Most patients wish to know their diagnosis,
even if it's fatal.

Many physicians prefer
to withhold this information.
And yet most of them reveal that
they would want to be told.

When dying people
are informed of their condition
they generally suffer
no negative consequences.

When they are *not* told the truth,

they are deprived
of free expression,
of shared understanding,
of putting their lives in order:
drawing a will, settling debts,
disposing of possessions.

By the conspiracy of silence,
they cannot share their fears and anxieties,
and be comforted.

They are "managed" like children,
stripped of self-determination and control.

Awareness opens communication
and allows choice;

choice encourages rational thinking;
rational thinking
reduces the fear of death.

The American Hospital Association
Patients' Bill of Rights
includes this:
    The patient has the right to obtain
from his physician complete current
information concerning his diagnosis,
treatment, and prognosis in terms the
patient can be reasonably expected to understand
. . . to give informed consent
prior to the start of any procedure
. . . and to refuse treatment
to the extent permitted by law.

WHO SHOULD TELL?

Usually the family physician,
but *never* on the telephone
(which occurs all too frequently).

Choose a time
when you can sit down
to talk together
without outside distraction.

After you hear the diagnosis,
share your understanding of the illness,
your reactions, fears, and feelings
about the condition, and
discuss the nature of the treatment.

There are no silly questions
when a loved one is dying.

HOW TO TELL

You hope your doctor will speak
simply,
gently,
balancing candor with kindness.

You or your loved one may hear the word
   "fatal"
and hear nothing else.

Later, when you are alone together,
try to recall and
clarify what you heard.

Be careful not to shut out your loved one
because you are so pained.

Another doctor's appointment may be scheduled
after you both have a chance
to absorb the bitter news.

Especially during difficult moments,
repetition
brings clarification and reinforcement.

WHAT TO TELL

The truth.
But truth is relative.

Some people can absorb it
only in small amounts.

Be sensitive to what your loved one
is or is not
asking.

People ordinarily do not face dying
with any more objectivity or serenity
than they have shown
during other life crises.

Nor should they be told in a way
that completely extinguishes hope.

But the hope
must be anchored in
realistic possibilities.

To speak of a "cure" encourages
false hope.

But,
pain *may* be reduced.
The life span *may* be extended
even beyond the doctor's expectations.

Frankness does not mean hopelessness.

Hope means different things
for different people
at different times.

Cancer patients hope before
the diagnosis
it won't be true.

But when it is,
they hope
they won't have too much pain.

And finally they may hope only
they'll live to see
a grandchild born.

Each hope is realistic—for the time.
Each new hope is tailored
to the new reality.

The greatest hope
is to live
as comfortably—as usefully—
as normally—as possible
for the remaining days:
to be valued, and
to be loved,
in the setting of
his or her choice.

*Hope is like the sun
which as we journey toward it
casts the shadow of our
burden behind us.*

—SAMUEL SMILES

III. YOUR LOVED ONE'S NEEDS

Of all things that move man, one
of the principle ones is the terror of death . . .
The idea of death, the fear of it,
haunts the human animal like
nothing else.

—ERNEST BECKER

Your loved one is *also*
in the throes
of anguish and agony.

It is a very understandable sorrow.

He or she is about to die.

> *"Light, light, the world needs
> more* light." *Goethe (on his deathbed)*

> *Many years later, the poet Unamuno wrote:*

>> *"Goethe was wrong; what he should have
>> said was* warmth. *The world needs more
>> warmth. We shall not die from the darkness
>> but from the cold."*

YOUR LOVED ONE'S EMOTIONAL NEEDS

The emotional requirements
of your loved one
may be harder
to understand and
tend to
than physical needs.

After all,
your loved one is
leaving all of the
places,
   people,
      things,
held dear over a lifetime.

Possibly losing social acceptance,
a sense of identity, and
a sense of dignity.

What torment it can be
to be suspended
between life and death!

DYING: A BREACH OF ETIQUETTE

A person known to be dying
may be ignored
by hospital personnel.

Priority is often given
to those whom they
might cure.

When doctors and nurses—
even family and friends—
see little hope for the patient's improvement,
they may withdraw from the dying person,
treating only the diseased organs
but not the person.

GUILT

You may be searching in your heart
for ways you have failed your loved one,
accusing yourself of negligence.

You may even lay the blame
for the illness
on an indiscretion or act
that occurred *before* the illness.

One man confided his
terrible feelings of recrimination—
attributing his wife's cancer
to his infidelity.

You may unrealistically
assume a power and
control
you simply do not possess.

You are suffering a guilt
that denies what you are—

a fallible human being.

You can't learn to love
unless you are willing to run the risk
of offending and failing.

You cannot love deeply
without occasionally hurting
the person you love.

All of us say and do things
we later regret.

There is always something more
we could have done.

Plaguing yourself with guilt
will not
make you or
your loved one better.

The fact that you may
blame yourself
demonstrates a concern
and a capacity
to feel for another.

PHYSICAL DISTRESS

Anxiety and fear create physical pain.

The strain of grieving in advance
causes physical distress.

Your mind can cause
changes in the way
your body works.

When feelings churn,
the stomach aches.

Food may have little taste
for you.

You eat only
because you think you should
—or you are pushed
to do it.

Or else,
you can't stop eating.

You constantly crave
a sugar or carbohydrate "fix"
to ease
an insatiable emotional hunger
to make your grief
more manageable.

You might also experience
long and torturous nights,
    an inability to sleep,
respiratory upsets,
    constant colds and sore throats.

Perhaps you have some of the symptoms
of your dying loved one.

You feel worn out and bedraggled.

Your body *is* feeling
the emotional loss.

The pain is not imagined.
It is *real*.

Strain adds to your risk
of ill health.

Check with your physician.
Have a physical examination.

If you can share with your doctor
not only your medical problems but
your emotional feelings and fears—
your body distress
may begin to diminish.

TEARS

"I can't stop crying.
   Am I losing control of myself?"

No.

You have every reason to weep.
Your loved one is dying.

Tears help to release emotions,
unlocking the tensions inside you.

Each person grieves in
his or her own way.

If you don't cry,
it should not be labeled
as "strength" or "bravery."

If you do cry,
it should not be described
as "weakness" or "cowardice."

Tears are healthy, normal ways
of coping.

They affirm your grief.

INTELLECTUALIZATION

Instead of emotional release,
often there are
words,
theories,
philosophical speculations.

Clinical and technical expressions
can cover up
your own real, intimate responses.

Certainly use information
for self-analysis.

But do not suffer paralysis
by analysis.

REPRIEVE

After you have begun to mourn,
then there is some improvement.
Your beloved takes a turn for the better.

You are unprepared.

You had *already* withdrawn
a part of yourself and
said your secret farewells.

There are mixed emotions
as you again include among the living
the person
you expected to be dead.

You are caught between
a tendency to *hang on*
and the inclination to *let go.*

Unsettled as you are by confused emotions,
you are coming to terms with impending loss—
understanding
that there is

no day without night, and

no hope without despair.

As you better *understand* yourself,
your anxiety and anguish,
as you begin to *accept* yourself,
even in your own insecurity,

you are better able to
understand and *accept*
your dying loved one
and respond to
his or her needs.

II. TERMINAL CANDOR
To Tell the Truth?

Truth is incontrovertible.
Panic may resent it;
ignorance may deride it;
malice may distort it;

but there it is.
　　　　　　　—WINSTON CHURCHILL

"I can't possibly tell my loved one
how sick he is.
It would destroy him.
He can't possibly handle
this terrible prognosis."

Maybe it is
you,

not your beloved,
who can't handle
and share the truth.

The question is not
whether or not
to tell of the
life-threatening illness,

but

who shall tell,
how to tell, and
what to tell.

The seriously ill can be placed in
a system of isolation,
treated as lepers.

The people who are dying
are cast into limbo,
depersonalized and dehumanized.

This only confirms their
primordial fears of
helplessness, hopelessness, and
abandonment.

Friends and family may say:
"I won't visit today.
It might be too tiring for my loved one.
Rest is so important."

It's one thing for a person
to *choose* to be alone.

It's quite another
to be *left* alone.

Dying people, too, may crave
companionship,
social acceptance, and
especially
emotional *warmth*.

They may see themselves
as rejected and discarded.

Often they *are!*

But they are afraid to share
their depression.

Family and friends may say
how well they're doing.
If patients respond with
the truth—
"They are not doing well at all"—

will their loved ones come back?

Loneliness may be more
fearsome
than even pain.

A SENSE OF IDENTITY

When family and friends retreat,
your loved one may have doubts
about his or her significance
and self-worth.

"I used to be a
parent,
  brother,
    sister,
      spouse,
        child,
          friend,
            person."

Relationships affirm identity.

"What am I now?
Do my family, friends, the hospital staff
see me only as
a *dying* patient?

    Yes, I'm dying.
    But I'm not dead yet.
    I'm still a living, breathing person
    with integrity and self-esteem.
    I need to be liked for myself.
    I need to live while I'm still alive."

A SENSE OF DIGNITY

"That means recognizing my needs
for self-worth,
    to live my life the way *I* want,
    as usefully and
    as normally
    as possible."

When death is expected,
family members may mistakenly believe
that their loved one
is no longer lucid and
is unable to discuss family matters

or
even to make decisions
about his or her own health care.

In your zeal to protect your loved one
from "unnecessary stress"
you may say:
"Don't worry.
Everything is being taken care of."

Your beloved is experiencing
a premortem death.

There is no dignity
when a *living* person
is left
for *dead.*

Allow your loved one to do the things
he or she *can* do,
and give encouragement
to do things
he or she *doesn't think* are possible.

Let your actions be based
on your beloved's needs,
not only on your own.

One dying person
wore a jersey in the hospital that read,

"Be patient,
God isn't finished with me yet."

As dying people
are able to recognize and resolve
many of their inner conflicts,
they become more at ease
with the idea of death.

They are more able
to face the prospect of death
with a sense of
acceptance and peace,

as long as
their physical needs
are also met.

YOUR LOVED ONE'S PHYSICAL NEEDS

It's not death, I fear,
but unspecified, unlimited pain."
—ROBERT LOWELL

Life refers to mind, spirit, and *body*.

Total care
means not only emotional comfort,
but control and relief of physical distress.

Good medical help is essential.

A PROPER DIAGNOSIS

The eminent psychiatrist Dr. Karl Menninger
asked his medical students for the most
significant part of the treatment process.

Some pupils referred to the skills
of the surgeon,
a few to bedside manner,
others to the revolution in drug therapy.

Dr. Menninger rejected all their answers.

His response was "a proper diagnosis."

If a patient is not correctly diagnosed,
he or she cannot be helped.

Many doctors have amazing skills and
knowledge in some areas.
But their wisdom may not extend to
all aspects of medical care.

The physician is an M.D.
not an M-Deity.

Very often the least-used words
in medicine are:
   "I don't know."
   "Let's find out."
   "I know where we might go to
   get some answers."

Don't be embarrassed
to ask for a consultation
with another doctor.

But *beware* of changing physicians regularly, or
flying around the country to assorted clinics.
This may demonstrate your *own* denial of the illness,
and could prevent your loved one
from participating in a consistent course of treatment.

A CARING PHYSICIAN

The word *diagnosis* derives from the Greek

 gignoskein—to know, *dia*—through and through

Choose a physician who will *know*
your loved one
as *through* and *through* as possible.

A health professional who will
STOP,
 LOOK, and
  LISTEN.

A doctor who will *stop*
to talk to you and your loved one,
not just walk into the room,
stand over your beloved for a brief moment,
mumble some technical phrases, and then
abruptly retreat,

look
at himself or herself with honesty as a physician,
not hiding behind the mask of professionalism,
admitting feelings of uncertainty and
not threatened by the limitations
of medicine to cure,

and *listen*

to what you and your loved one
have to say, and
not treat you as irresponsible children.

A secure, caring physician allows
and encourages
participation in meaningful decisions.

Obviously, just as there are
no all-perfect people
so there can be
no all-perfect physician.

A doctor who meets
the needs of one person splendidly
can be totally ineffectual
with another.

Determine with your family physician
which specialist
would give your loved one
the medical care that is needed
and would understand as well
your beloved's
likes and dislikes,
concerns and fears,
hopes and desires—

who would know the person of the patient.

CONTROL OF PAIN AND SUFFERING

One of the most common errors,
is the notion that pain and dying
are inseparable companions.
The truth is that they rarely go together.
Occasionally, the act of dissolution
is a painful one,
but this should be the exception to
the general rule.

—EDWARD CLARKE, Visions, 1878

Pain is not only physical,
it is psychological as well.

Whether pain is bearable
may depend upon the meaning
a person gives to it.

Everyone has a
different
tolerance for pain.

Drug therapy is often administered
to relieve suffering.

New discoveries in pharmacology
help many patients
live through their final days
without undue discomfort and torment.

The patients often know
their *own* need for drugs.

Too often medicines are given
before they are requested,
before they are needed.

Drugs should not be so administered
to distort reality or
alter the state of consciousness.

Using drugs for the convenience
of the staff
is *drug abuse.*

Speak to your doctor.

Share your observations
of your loved one's response to the medication
and inquire
whether the dosage is appropriate
for your loved one's *present* condition and
whether other drugs
or none at all
may *now* be indicated.

The purpose of the medication
is to make patients' lives
as bearable as possible,
and help them to go on living
as themselves.

Treatment can become overtreatment.

To artificially prolong life
with heroic measures, when
the pain is great, and
the death is imminent,

may not be in the best interest
of your loved one.

Dying people, too, demand dignity.
They may want to die while they're
still themselves.

IV. YOUR CHILDREN'S NEEDS

A child is as sensitive
to outside influences and forces
as a seismograph is sensitive
to an earthquake
which is ten thousand miles away.

—LUTHER BURBANK

You are not the only one affected
by impending loss.

Children are often forgotten by grieving adults.

Having a loved one who will soon die
is potentially destructive to their health.

Sorrow leaves an imprint on
the healthiest of personalities.

Be truthful.

Explain to them,
in words they can understand,
what the problem is,
why you are not as available to them as before,
and why your moods are so changeable.

Silence and secrecy
heighten their sense of being shut out
and isolated
from reality.

If possible,
allow them to visit, too.
They are part of the family.

You will be surprised at the
cheering effect they will
have on your loved one.

The role of children
can be pivotal
in a dying person's ability
to feel alive.

Prepare them in advance
for what the person will look like—
with wounds or sores or hair and weight loss,
with tubes, a respirator, or
other medical equipment.

Children need not be harmed emotionally
by visiting the seriously ill.

What they see is rarely so bad
as what they fear might be.

They may learn that mental health
is not the denial of tragedy,
but the frank acknowledgment of it.

A visit can prepare them for the future.

Help them understand that
the world of biology
is the world of living *and* dying.

V. FINAL SETTINGS
Where to Die?

*One hour well spent, when a man's
life is almost outspent,
may gain a man the assurance of eternal life.*

—ARS MORIENDI (Book on
the Art of Dying
Lewis Bayly, *The Practice of
Pietie*, written 1612

Years ago, most people were nursed at home,
and died there.

Death took place in the midst of kin,
with the comfort of familiar surroundings.

Today, most people die
in institutions.

The French social historian Philippe Aries
describes the trend as
   "a brutal revolution in traditional ideas
   and feelings."

Most people
would choose to die at home,
in an environment of continuity and security,
having the greatest possible control
over their lives,

not treated as dying patients,
but as living people.

Many ill people and their families
are unaware
that dying at home
can be a real option.

There are resources.
Hospital out-patient departments,
medical and nursing services
can provide help for
your beloved at home.

Relatives and friends can be taught
how to care effectively for the loved one and
how to administer drugs at home.

Homemaker and sitter services
will allow you some respite
from constant care.

You may benefit, *too*,
if you care for your
dying loved one.

You are giving a gift of
your time,
your self,
your familiar touch.

Sharing your
burdens, joys and last hours together
may draw you closer
and ease your burdens
of helplessness and guilt.

Institutions can distance dying people
when
they may spend their final days
in sterile settings,
sharing accommodations with strangers,
managed by institutional personnel,
rather than family.

Often, they die lonely deaths,
neither dignified nor tranquil.

The bureaucratization of death
can have a high psychological cost.

But home care is
not always possible or desirable.

Don't feel guilty
if it isn't feasible for your family.

The sick person
may become confused, disoriented, and
in need of medical and psychological care
not available
outside of a hospital facility.

When a loved one is dying,
family members may be torn
between responsibility for the sick person
and for
the other members of the household.

The unity of the home is disrupted
when the members
can *no longer* accept the added tension
of a crisis situation
and feelings, formerly controlled,
explode.

Pressures—physical, emotional, and social—
may be unbearable,
particularly if the illness
has been a lingering one.

Frustration and fatigue
can deplete the strength
of the most loving and devoted person.

Weigh all the choices.
Take time to decide.
Seek support of other
family members, including
the dying person—
if you can.

HOSPITALS AND NURSING HOMES

When home care is not feasible,
hospitals and nursing homes
may be appropriate places for your loved one.

Check carefully the reputation,
facilities, and personnel of
any hospital or nursing home
you consider.

Look for

smaller, specialized wards,
offering individualized treatment.

Even in a large facility,
you can find intimacy and
warmth.

Surround your loved one with
familiar things
that he or she values.

Decorate the room with personal items.
Arrange to bring in favorite foods occasionally.

See if your beloved
could conveniently wear his or her own nightclothes
rather than the usual hospital garb.

Don't be surprised if your
requests are denied—and don't
give up.

Be quietly persistent.

Speak to the administrator, if necessary,
to get an adequate reason
for the refusal—or a
reversal of policy.

Throughout the country,
families and friends
are challenging the
once sacred
institutional rules, regulations, and
visiting policies that
isolate them
from their loved one's
last days of life.

Long-established rules
are being revised.

Small children may be allowed to
visit the dying person.
Visiting hours have become more flexible.

Patients or their families
may participate in planning and
carrying out of care.

As closely as possible, attempt
to provide
the kind of loving care
that you would give
at home.

THE HOSPICE IDEA

Since 1967, another setting
has been available for the dying person.

Historically, a hospice
was both hospital and hotel.
Pilgrims could stop there
for rest and sustenance.

Today, the hospice
is a place for respite
but not cure.

In St. Christopher's in England
the wards are noted for
their spaciousness and peaceful atmosphere.
Big windows fill the hospice with light.
There are flowers everywhere.

Visitors come
whenever they like,
stay as long as they want
but never on Monday—
Monday is "relatives day off."
The hairdresser comes,
and the hospice holds parties and concerts.

In the dining room
patients, visitors, staff and their children
(yes, there is a day-care center at the hospice)
gather for meals.

Patients are allowed to make decisions,
read when they want,
eat in the garden at their leisure,
keep their own clothes,
bring a familiar chair from home.

The hospice staff extends home visiting
with an out-patient team of
cooperative physicians, nurses, clergy, and
social workers.

The patients' final days
are free of pain.
No heroic resuscitations
are undertaken.
There is a skillful tailoring
of medication
to individual needs.

No wonder then
that hundreds of hospices,
each with varying approaches,
—some with home care and some in hospitals—
are springing up all over America.

They can create a warm, accommodating
atmosphere
for family and friends
to say a loving "goodbye."

The hospice is an idea
whose time has come.

VI. HELPING YOURSELF

If I am not for myself,
Who will be for me?
　　　　　　　　—HILLEL

Caring for a dying person
is a demanding responsibility.

You just cannot devote
every minute
of every day
to vigilant watchfulness
over your loved one.

You need time.

TO RELAX EMOTIONALLY

In times of stress,
it is important that
you continue to live your life
as normally as possible.

You need interludes of emotional,
physical, and spiritual rest,
some space for

respite,
reprieve, and
re-creation.

Try to find a quiet time for yourself
each day,
even "five-minute vacations."
Wind down and try to relax.

There is healing in solitude.

A little withdrawal from
the constant tension
allows you to return to your beloved
refreshed, renewed, restored

—a little different—
from the distraught person you were.

Alcohol and drugs may seem to be
the instant relaxation you need
to ease your fears and anxieties.

Wait.

You are only smothering
your pain artificially.

Drugs have built-in dangers.

They may:
Delay your grief.
Deepen your depression.
Become addictive.

Sedation is no cure
for grief.

Overbusyness can lure
you away
from facing your pain.

*I must lose myself in action
lest I wither in despair.*
—TENNYSON, after the death
of his friend Arthur Hallam

There are dangers.
When activities reach a frenzied pitch,
the body gives way to exhaustion.

You need time . . .

TO RELAX PHYSICALLY

More than ever
you should try to stay healthy.

Do not skip meals.
Proper nutrition is vital.

Regular exercise releases pent-up feelings
and keeps your body strong.
Sufficient sleep fights physical fatigue.

You must maintain your health
if you are to effectively take care of
your beloved.

Just as important as it is for you
to be alone,
so you
need time . . .

TO SHARE WITH FRIENDS

"I have so much on my mind.
Just doing those things that need to be done
consumes my every moment.
I can't think of being with anyone else."

Yes, you are tired and weary.
But you need other people
like never before.

Don't escape into loneliness.

Share with trusted friends
your thoughts and fears.

Choose carefully those friends
who will accept and understand,
who will not fault you
or deny your feelings.

Emotions that are denied expression
grow in isolation.

People need people
and friends need friends
because we *all* need love.

Don't "lock up your hearts"
and fail to heed
the outstretched hand of
a kindred spirit,
willing to share your burdens.

As you relax physically and
emotionally
consider also
a time . . .

TO RELAX SPIRITUALLY

Perhaps more than any other event
the impending loss of a loved one
raises the most urgent issues
about

good and evil,
reward and punishment,
a theology of an afterlife.

Your religion may provide you
with a spiritual philosophy
that helps you make some sense of
death and life.

Beware.

Religion can be hazardous to your health,
when you believe you haven't prayed hard enough,
and punishment is linked with death.

Religion then becomes a tool
for denial of real emotions and
keeps you from releasing feelings of
helplessness, guilt, anger.

A mature, forgiving, open faith
sustains these feelings,
encourages expression,
allows your angry cry to heaven—
  "How could You, God?"

Religion offers: no absolute answers,
no guarantee of special treatment,
no extended length of time for your beloved.

For many,
faith *does* offer

a glimpse
beyond the fragile, transient life
on earth,
of an eternal life—
of happiness and peace,

and helps its believers
to accept the unacceptable.

VII. HELPING YOUR LOVED ONE

To everything, there is a season
and a time to every purpose
under the heaven.

—ECCLESIASTES

A TIME TO VISIT

Dying is one task that
each person must perform
entirely by himself or herself.

That is not to say
that your loved one
should die *alone*.

Visit frequently,
if your loved one is not at home.

Share news of the family.

Seek your beloved's advice,
so he or she will know that
his or her judgment *still* is valued.

Bring small gifts.

Especially bring yourself.

You may find it painful
visiting a dying person,
especially someone with an advanced disease.

When a loved one's features
change markedly
it is hard to believe
you are with the same person.

It is difficult to keep eye contact.
Words don't come easily.

You try to act naturally,
but you feel awkward.

Suddenly, your beloved
seems a stranger.

Think of the person
you knew.
Inside he or she's probably
the same.

"Real isn't how you are made," said the Skin Horse.
"It's a thing that happens to you."
"Does it hurt?" asked the Rabbit.
"Sometimes," said the Skin Horse, for he was always
truthful.
"When you are Real, you don't mind being hurt.
It doesn't often happen to people who break easily, or
have sharp edges, or who have to be carefully kept.
Generally, by the time you are Real, most of your hair
has been loved off, and your eyes drop out, and you
get loose in the joints and very shabby. But these
things don't matter at all, because once you are Real,
you can't be ugly, except to people who don't
understand."

—MARGARITE WILLIAMS, *The Velveteen Rabbit*

A TIME TO TALK

Not with—
  "Snap out of it.
  Everything will be fine, you'll see.
  Try to get hold of yourself."
Chattering isn't communication.

Neither is denial.

Your loved one doesn't need
platitudes and reassurances
that you both
know are false.

They signal your beloved
not to share, but
to hide
real fear and feelings
from you.

Don't try to make life "normal"
by pretending nothing is wrong.

The dying person
to talk not only
but about
the life that is pa

A loved one ne
that his or her lif
did have an imp

Consider:
a tape recorder o
to be *forever* chr

Or an album of p
and of keepsake s

These records of
reduce feelings of
meaninglessness

At the same time
avoid saying
"terminal" or "helpless."

Such words make the dying person feel
written off
the rolls of the living.

Stress
that you and the doctors
will do all you can
to make your loved one comfortable.

Look your loved one in the eye.
Be open and straightforward.

You allow an
honest exchange of feelings
when you say:
    "It must be hard for you. Is it not so?
    I'd like to help you, but I
    don't know what to do—
    what would you suggest?"

Don't be afraid of admitting
    your anxiety
    your indecision, and
    your pain.

Even though no one
can truly understand
another person's feelings,
try to empathize and
identify your loved one's feelings.

Ask yourself:
  "Knowing my beloved like I do,
  aware that life will be cut short,
  how would I react
  if it were I?"

The dying person may feel a need
to talk not only about death,
but about
the life that is past.

A loved one needs to know
that his or her life on earth
did have an impact upon others.

Consider:
a tape recorder of the life for an oral history
to be *forever* chronicled.

Or an album of pictures
and of keepsakes.

These records of one's life
reduce feelings of
meaninglessness and absurdity.

A TIME TO LISTEN

During moments of crisis,
many people are so concerned
about *what* to say,
that they frame answers
without hearing what is said.

More important than your words
is your ability to listen
not only to what is said,
but how it is said
and what is meant, and

to seize the secret messages of silence.

Listen between the lines—
emotional content, body language,
silences, avoided topics.

Eyes averted,
turned-down head,
posture-shifts,
the tone of voice

may speak louder than words.

Allow full expression of
fears and nightmares.
    "Will there be torturous pain . . .?
    Will I suffocate . . .?"

Tell your loved one:
    "It is normal to express these feelings.
    I'm glad you shared your thoughts with me.
    Didn't the doctor assure you that . . ."

Dying may be a time
when courage runs quite thin and faith
is but a theological abstraction.

Have the courage to listen to things
that are not always pleasant to hear.

Sometimes, all that is needed
is your being there,

and saying nothing.

Rather than a forced conversation
the best communication
may be a thoughtful silence, and
a tender touch.

A dying woman said:
    "The person who helped me the most
    said very little.
    But I knew by his look and his manner
    that he knew what I was experiencing.
    There was an "I know" meeting of
    two hearts, especially
    when I saw tears glisten in his eyes."

A TIME TO CRY

Tears are wordless messages,
a vital part of grieving:

Pain can be eased
when people are able
to weep together.

Friends and family
may believe that
crying *in front of*
or *with* a dying person
will be upsetting to the loved one.

Not true.

A dying child said to her parents:
   "Aren't you sad that I'm so sick?
   Don't you care?
   How come I've never seen you cry?"

A TIME TO TOUCH

Sickness can make a person
feel very lonely and apart.

A dying person needs more than ever
to be close to the living.

The sense of touch
reduces the bleakest of all feelings—
abandonment.

Holding your loved one communicates:
"No matter how serious the illness,
feelings toward me have not changed:
   I am not rejected.
   I am not untouchable."

Don't be afraid to reach out physically:
a warm embrace,
a firm handshake, a pat on the shoulder,
the gentle stroking of the forehead,
a soothing and comforting massage . . .

When words fail,
the touch of reassurance is vital.

Hugging, holding, kissing
may be the best medicine
for your loved one
and for you.

They say:

"I love you."

A TIME TO LAUGH

Dying people need
lightness and smiles in their lives.

People who have a good sense of
humor during their lifetimes

often maintain their sense of humor
in their dying.

Somberness
won't make you or your loved one better.

A dying person quipped:
    "My situation is hopeless
    but not serious."

Humor helped her manage feelings
that were too great to deal with openly.

The threat of her future
was no less menacing,
but it became easier to bear.

Laughing together
is one of the normal ways
that people relate to each other.

One patient said to a chaplain:

> "You've become so morbid and gloomy
> since you heard my prognosis.
> You used to tell me such humorous
> stories.
> I'm the same person that I was
> before the diagnosis.
> How come you aren't fun anymore?"

VIII. HELPING EACH OTHER

*Life is not a matter
of holding good cards,
but playing a poor hand
well.*

—ROBERT LOUIS STEVENSON

The fact that one person's heart will stop beating
doesn't mean
that another person's heart will stop loving.

Would you trade in
your life's experiences with your beloved
because of all
the pain and anguish you are having now?

Your love can now
grow
knowing the limits of time, or
diminish
because of the pain of impending loss.

This is your real choice in anticipating grief—
to *grow* or
to *diminish*.

"All persons are mortal.
I am a person.
Therefore, I am mortal.
(But I don't believe it.)"

Now you are *beginning*
to realize your mortal nature,
as you watch your loved one die.

The slogan
"Today is the first day
of the rest of your life"
is but a half-truth.

Now you know the other half.

"Today may also be the last day
you'll ever get."

When you face your own death realistically, you will, perhaps:

- ☐ plan for or revise your will,
- ☐ consider funeral procedures and arrangements for interment,
- ☐ design a program of insurance and planning for your estate,
- ☐ contact the social security office to update your death benefit account,
- ☐ put your important papers in order.

In short, when you actually
prepare for that inevitable moment,
you will then see your life differently.

There is a noticeable shift in your priorities,
an intensive soul-searching for new meanings,
and the use of your energy for
what is really important
in your life.

Death makes life precious.

You realize that the two *least*
important details
are usually inscribed upon the tombstone
—dates of birth and death.

You will not be remembered
for the *length* of your years, but
     the *breadth* of your sympathies for others,
     the *depth* of your appreciation for beauty,
     the *height* of your love.

Through this personal transformation,
you experience an opportunity for growth
by *shedding* those attitudes
which prevent you
from living life—
strengthening those qualities
which add depth to your being.

As you work through your grief,
you become aware
of the treasures
which comprise life.

The big things in life
suddenly become small,
the small things
very large.

You are setting new priorities.
Sometimes the simple things of life
become the most enjoyable.

You may not be afraid of
your death in itself,
but of the incompleteness of your life.

Love is stronger than the grave.

—SONG OF SONGS

You know that your love
for your dear one
will never die
even after death.

There are golden days you will never forget.

Love has no rigid bounds.
Love goes beyond the self,
beyond a precious loved one,
flowing freely,
reaching out
touching, as it flows.

Love is hard,
but
it makes everything else easier.

In the midst of death
your loved one is helping you
to confront life,
finding

    sympathy in your sorrow,
    comfort in your crisis,
    acceptance in your anguish, and
    love in your loneliness.

A final thought:

A little boy confused his prayer,
saying:

> "Now I lay me down to sleep,
> I pray the Lord my soul to keep,
> if I should die
> before I . . .
> *live.*"

The real tragedy is
to *die*
before you *live.*

One woman said—

> "Having to face the fact
> that my husband is dying
> makes us value our love
> with an intensity and intimacy
> that we had never known before.
> Each day becomes a gift
> to experience together—
> No longer do we take our
> relationship for *granted*."

As you discover so much
about your beloved—
the hurts, fears, hopes—

so are you learning
so much about yourself.

You must confront dying
before you can successfully
confront living.

Each day is another day of life
to be enjoyed together
as fully as you can.

Try not to think it's just another day
closer to death.

> There is no cure for birth or death,
> Save to enjoy the interlude.

–GEORGE SANTAYANA

LOOK TO THIS DAY

Look to this day,
For it is life.
The very life of life,
In its brief course lies all
The realities and verities
*   of existence . . .*

For yesterday is but a dream,
And tomorrow is only a vision.
But today well lived,
Makes every day a dream
*   of happiness,*
And every tomorrow a vision
*   of hope.*
Look well, therefore, to this day.

—SANSKRIT PROVERB

IX. WHERE TO GO FOR HELP

SELF-HELP GROUPS

Many people who have experienced the dying of a loved one have developed tremendous gifts of insight. They understand the value of sharing. They may help you reach out of your isolation to a meaningful support system.

Self-help groups may provide the emotional intervention in working through your fears and frustrations. They also serve as a learning resource in providing knowledge about the disease and assisting you to cope with daily health problems. Fellow sufferers often become second families to each other.

CANDLELIGHTERS An international organization of parents whose children have had cancer. Formed in 1970, there are today over 120 groups located in 48 states and in Canada, England, France, and Australia. A statement from a Candlelighters publication summarizes the organization's focus: "Candlelighters parents share the shock of diagnosis, the questions about treatment, the anxiety of waiting, the despair of relapse, the grief of death, the despondency of loss, the hope of remission, the joy of cure."

In addition to its monthly meetings and other planned activities, the chapter participates in national programs to promote concern and awareness of the problem of childhood cancer and research into its cause and cure. Write:

123 C Street SE
Washington, DC 20003

COMPASSIONATE FRIENDS A support group for bereaved parents who "need not walk alone. We are Compassionate Friends—people who care and share and listen to each other." Group discussions range from helping the grieving accept death to handling family holidays after the death of a child.

P.O. Box 1347
Oak Brook, Illinois 60521

MAKE TODAY COUNT An international organization for persons with life-threatening illnesses, their families and other interested persons. In the words of the organization's founder, Orville Kelly, "I do not look upon each day as another day closer to death, but as another day of life, to be appreciated and enjoyed."

The original group of eighteen members was formed in 1974 in Burlington, Iowa. Make Today Count now has more than 210 chapters in the United States, West Germany, Canada, and Australia.

P.O. Box 303
Burlington, Iowa 52601

NRTA—AARP—AIM The National Retired Teachers Association, the American Association of Retired Teachers, and Action for Independent Maturity (NRTA—AARP—AIM) jointly form a network for living through bereavement. An outreach program helps those on a one-to-one basis, as well as those in larger group sessions, with a telephone service for referral information, a public education program for family adjustment, and counseling for financial and legal affairs.

1909 K Street NW
Washington, DC 20049

SHARE AND CARE Representatives of nursing, social services, and chaplaincy staffs foster close relationships among cancer patients and family members who become involved with each other's problems during weekly meetings. The group is encouraged to visit its members who are hospitalized or homebound due to their illnesses. Spouses often continue to come to the meetings after a patient dies. Through continued contact with the group, survivors share their grief experiences and help others who may be facing similar problems.

Cancer Education Coordinator
North Memorial Medical Center
3220 Lowry Avenue North
Minneapolis, Minnesota 55422

MAJOR MEDICAL INFORMATION SERVICES

AMERICAN CANCER SOCIETY Services for cancer patients include information and referral, transportation and nursing services (on a limited basis depending upon the resources of the county unit). Hospital equipment often is loaned to patients who wish to go home but require special facilities.

In addition to these general services, the society sponsors trained visitor programs, "Reach to Recovery" and the "Ostomy Rehabilitation Program."

The Reach to Recovery rehabilitation program is designed to help women who have undergone mastectomy deal with their new physical, psychological, and cosmetic needs.

A similar program is offered for new ostomates. Well-adjusted volunteers who have had their ostomies for a period of time are carefully trained in a course of lectures, films, simulated interviews, and supervised hospital visits.

The International Association of Laryngectomees, sponsored by the American Cancer Society, offers psychological support to new laryngectomees and their families.

777 Third Avenue
New York, NY 10017

The Cancer Information Service is another resource agency for a wide variety of questions regarding carcinogens, treatment, diagnosis, and community resources. Services available in twenty-two states. If not listed in your directory, call 1–800–638–6694.

AMERICAN HEART ASSOCIATION Provides information about heart disease as well as specialized services for home-making and home nursing services and facilities for heart patients.

44 East 23rd Street
New York, NY 10010

AMERICAN LUNG ASSOCIATION State associations provide informal services to dying persons and their families.

147

Most associations also offer patient-family education programs for persons with chronic lung diseases such as emphysema, chronic bronchitis, and asthma.

LEUKEMIA SOCIETY OF AMERICA An outreach program for patients diagnosed with leukemia, Hodgkin's disease, and lymphoma.
  In some areas, transportation and payment of certain drugs not covered by individual insurance are supplied.

> 211 East 43rd Street
> New York, NY 10017

NATIONAL COMMITTEE ON THE TREATMENT OF INTRACTABLE PAIN Promotes education and research on more effective management and relief of unbearable pain.

> P.O. Box 34571
> Washington, DC 20034

RIGHT TO DIE AND LIVING WILL The Council of Concern for Dying has created a document called "A Living Will" when "If the time comes when I can no longer take part in decisions for my own future . . . if the situation should arise in which there is no reasonable expectation of my recovery from physical or mental disability, I request that I be allowed to die and not be kept alive by artificial means or heroic measures." The purpose of the Living Will is to relieve the physicians' specific responsibility as a preserver of life when the patient's sickness becomes so intolerable that death is looked upon as a healing and merciful act.
  Passive euthanasia—the withholding of extraordinary treatment—has generally been upheld.

> 250 West 57th Street
> New York, NY 10019

PERSONAL SERVICES

FINAL DISPOSITION For choosing a cemetery on a pre-need basis so decisions may be made under the most normal emotional circumstances, contact:

American Cemetery Association
250 East Broad Street
Columbus, Ohio 43215

Cremation Association of North America
15300 Ventura Blvd., Suite 305
Sherman Oaks, California 91403

National Association of Cemeteries
1911 North Forest Meyer Drive, Suite 409
Arlington, Virginia 22209

National Catholic Cemetery Conference
710 North River Road
Des Plaines, Illinois 60016

COUNSELING For help during the difficult period, consult your local mental health clinic, the family service association, or contact:

Psychological:
American Psychological Association
1200 17th Street NW
Washington, DC 20036

Psychiatric:

American Psychiatric Association 1700 18th Street NW Washington, DC 20009	American Psychoanalytic Association 1 East 57th Street New York, NY 10022

Social Work:
National Association of Social Workers
1425 H Street NW
Washington, DC 20005

A note of caution: Not all mental health workers are skilled in bereavement counseling.

FINANCIAL For economic assistance and advice, consult your local telephone directory under "United States Government" for the appropriate federal agencies such as:

Office of Children—funds to help cover child care costs

Social Security Office

Council on Aging or Elder Affairs Department

Veterans Administration

Emergency funds and facilities may also be obtained from your municipal or state department of social services. Look in your telephone directory under "Social Services" and "Welfare Agencies."

FUNERAL If you have not given some thought to funeral arrangements before they are necessary, you may find it difficult to consider the many details at the time of final separation. The pamphlet "Preparing Today for the Eventual Tomorrow" is invaluable and includes a check list of other pamphlets and helpful books. Write:

The National Funeral Directors Association
135 West Wells Street
Milwaukee, Wisconsin 53203

HOMEMAKER SERVICE For food shopping, personal errands, light housekeeping, and assistance in hygienic duties, such as giving baths, changing dressings, and helping with prescribed exercises, consult your local telephone directory under "Homemaker" or "Home Service Aide," your local social service department, or

TRANSPORTATION For the patient who may need personal assistance to visit the doctor or clinic, when public transportation is unavailable or inaccessible, consult your local social service department.

HEALTH SERVICES

BLOOD DONATION For blood donations and transportation services consult your telephone directory under "Red Cross" or your local health department, or contact:

The American National Red Cross
National Headquarters
Washington, DC 20006

HOSPICE For further understanding of the hospice movement in helping not only the dying patient but supporting the family as a unit of care, contact:

HOSPICE, Inc.
765 Prospect Street
New Haven, Connecticut 06511

Hospice of Marin
Kentfield, California 94904

Saint Christopher's Hospice
51–53 Lawrie Park Road
Sydenham, London SE26 6DZ
United Kingdom

NURSING For vital nursing needs, consult your telephone directory under "Visiting Nurse" and "Nursing Association" or your local health department, or contact:

National League for Nursing
10 Columbus Drive
New York, NY 10019

NURSING HOME   For information regarding nursing homes contact:

American Health Care Association
1025 Connecticut Avenue NW
Washington, DC 20036
Represents commercial nursing homes.

American Association of Homes for the Aging
529 14th Street NW
Washington, DC 20004
Represents nonprofit home for the aging.

ORGAN DONATION   For a vital organ for the ill or a donation at the time of death, the Uniform Anatomical Gift Act is now law in 50 states. Advances in medical science now make it possible to replace a variety of malfunctioning organs. Techniques for transplanting kidneys and corneas are currently the most advanced, but progress is being made in other areas such as liver, pancreas, heart, bone, and other tissue. A donated organ successfully transplanted is literally the gift of life. For further information, consult your physician or

National Kidney Foundation
2 Park Avenue
New York, NY 10016

REHABILITATION   For the patients' physical therapy and rehabilitation, consult your telephone directory under "Rehabilitation Services" or contact:

American Physical Therapy Association
1740 Broadway
New York, NY 10019

Association of Rehabilitation Facilities
5530 Wisconsin Avenue NW
Washington, DC 20015